CONTENTS

THROWING IT AWAY

A chef at a restaurant sweeps his hand across the worktop. Lemon peel, bits of chicken and bread crumbs fall into his hand. He throws them in the bin. A woman on the street carries a plastic bag from a shop. She throws a sweet wrapper into a dustbin as she walks by. A child throws an empty yoghurt pot in a bin.

The journey of rubbish can begin anywhere. It usually ends at the landfill. Some rubbish **decomposes** at the landfill. But not all rubbish ends up there. Some rubbish is **littered** and ends up where it doesn't belong.

decompose break down into smaller pieces

litter throw rubbish in a place where it does not belong, allowing it to end up in water or on land

Depending on what the rubbish is and where it ends up, it can take between 1 week and an estimated 1 million years for it to decompose.

People throw many things away.

CHAPTER ONE

RUBBISH AT THE LANDFILL

Things become rubbish when they go into a bin. The rubbish can be there for several days before someone takes it away. A bin lorry collects the rubbish. The lorries take the rubbish to the landfill.

One type of rubbish is **organic** waste, which includes recyclable rubbish. Examples of organic waste include pizza crusts, orange peels, paper and cardboard. Another type of rubbish includes plastic, metal containers and glass items. Rubbish is sorted at a landfill. Things that can be reused are saved. The rest is dumped in the landfill.

organic made of material that was once living

Landfills are giant waste storage areas.

In a landfill, rubbish is dumped into a large hole in the ground. Some decomposes while it sits there. Decomposition is the process of breaking something down and changing it into simpler forms.

FACT

The largest landfill in the United States is in New York. It was filled from 1948 to 2001. It was 6 kilometres (4 miles) wide and 154 metres (505 feet) deep when it closed.

Anaerobes are too small for the human eye to see.

Anaerobes break down organic waste. Anaerobes are **microorganisms**. They work best in areas without air. Organic waste decomposes into gases. Metals, glass and plastic break up slowly into small pieces. Anaerobes do not make them decompose.

The landfill hole has a liner. The liner lets very little liquid through. Beneath the liner is a layer of clay. The clay helps **absorb** unsafe chemicals, stopping them from leaking into the soil.

microorganism living thing that is too small to be seen without a microscope

absorb take in water

Several centimetres of soil are put between the layers of rubbish. The soil helps control the smell. It also protects the air. The layers absorb the landfill gas. Some landfills have pipes connected to them. The pipes collect landfill gas. The gas is burned to become energy for nearby cities.

Landfills protect people and Earth. They are located in areas without many people or animals. They are the end of the cycle for rubbish that is thrown away. However, too much rubbish is thrown into landfills. About 70 per cent of waste in a landfill could be recycled or **composted**.

compost recycle organic matter so it becomes fertile soil

CHAPTER **TWO**

ORGANIC
WASTE

Organic waste is made of material that was once living. It decomposes fairly quickly. Microorganisms, water and sunlight break down organic waste. First, water, wind and other forces break the waste into smaller pieces. Once the pieces are small, microorganisms break them down. Microorganisms change the waste into gases and **minerals**. Eventually, the organic waste becomes part of the soil. This natural process creates nutrients for the soil and air.

mineral material found in nature that is not an animal or plant

Different types of organic waste decompose at different rates.

Most organic waste in landfills takes months or years to break down. Newspaper takes about six weeks to decompose. Cardboard takes about two months.

Composting is a great way to reuse organic waste.

→ COMPOSTING

Composting is a natural process. It is a way to recycle organic matter such as food and garden waste. Some people compost in their gardens. It can be done in a barrel or container. Organic matter gives off heat while it breaks down. Decomposition can take two months to two years. The compost can be used as fertile soil.

Pieces of wood can take one to three years. Wool clothing takes one to five years.

It is not good for organic waste to sit in landfills. It cannot release nutrients back to the soil. It should be composted. Composting is when aerobic microorganisms decompose organic waste. They break down waste, but they need air. Landfills are covered, so there is little or no air. In composting, the waste turns into nutrients for the soil. It helps plants to grow.

→ **fertile** having lots of nutrients to help plants grow better

Paper is often tied in bales to be recycled.

Some organic waste can be recycled. It can be reused. It may go through many uses before ending up in a landfill. Paper and cardboard are the

FACT Three times more paper is recycled than is sent to landfills.

most commonly recycled materials. Shoe boxes, cereal boxes and paper from notebooks can all be recycled. They can also be composted.

The process starts when items are taken to recycling facilities. They are sorted by paper type and weight. Then they go to the paper mill. They are mixed with water. The water breaks up the paper into slurry. Slurry is a mix of paper pieces and water. Next, the mix is spread onto cloth or wire. As it dries, more layers are put on. It is dried in rolls. The rolls can weigh as much as 2 tonnes. Finally, it is ready to be turned into a new product.

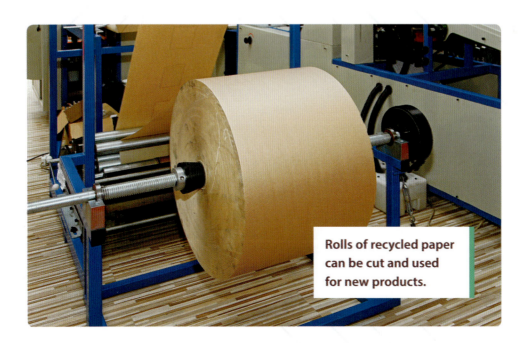

Rolls of recycled paper can be cut and used for new products.

CHAPTER THREE

PLASTIC, GLASS AND METALS

Plastic, glass and metals take years to degrade. Degrading is a process where rubbish breaks into smaller and smaller pieces. It never completely goes away.

Glass is used for bottles, mirrors and more. Plastic is shaped into food containers and water bottles. Nappies have plastic in them too. Electronic devices such as phones are made of plastic, glass and metal parts. Drinks cans are metal. All these materials last many years.

Plastic, glass and metal rubbish do not decompose. It takes a long time for them to break up.

Plastic is made from small organic molecules bonded together. It is water resistant and strong. The bonds are difficult to break down. Plastic doesn't typically break down into small, useful parts. It just breaks up into smaller pieces of plastic.

The type of plastic determines how quickly it breaks up. The process can happen in days or many hundreds of years. Styrofoam is a foamed plastic made of tiny beads. It takes more than 50 years for Styrofoam to break up. A plastic bag may take 450 years to break up. In the ocean, plastic may take 80 to 200 years to break up. But scientists cannot observe such long processes. They do not know exactly how long these processes actually take.

Plastic bags harm wildlife and the environment.

RECYCLING PLASTIC

Plastic goes to a recycling facility to make it ready for reuse. In one method, workers sort it into similar types. Machines shred the plastic into tiny bits. Paper labels and other things are washed off the plastic. Another machine melts the plastic. The plastic is formed into small pellets. It is easy to make pellets into new shapes.

Plastic has to be exposed to sunlight to break up. Sunlight weakens the bonds slowly over time. First, the thin outer layer weakens. Water and air can then reach the surface of the plastic. The water and air help break the bonds, layer by layer. Finally, the plastic degrades into smaller and smaller pieces. Chemicals are released when the bonds break. They can **pollute** water or soil where the plastic is degrading.

FACT

About 2 million plastic bags are used around the world every minute.

pollute make water, air or land dirty and potentially harmful to living things nearby

Glass can be made in different ways. One common glass is made by mixing lime, **silica** and **sodium carbonate** at very high temperatures. Glass can be man-made or found in nature. It is extremely strong. It resists heat, water and bacteria. It takes the longest of all materials to break up. Glass that is more than 1,500 years old has been found in Israel. Scientists think it could take more than 1 million years for glass bottles to break up.

A glass jar from hundreds of years ago can appear hardly changed.

silica part of sand
sodium carbonate chemical that can be used to make glass

When glass breaks up, the outer layer absorbs some water and flakes off. However, modern glass is made very carefully. The outer layer may only slightly flake.

The best option for glass is to recycle it. It can be crushed into small pieces. It is then melted and shaped into new products.

Glass is crushed during the recycling process so it melts easily.

RECYCLING METALS

Metal is recycled in a similar way to other materials. It is shredded, melted and reused. Small cans aren't the only recycled metals. Metal from cars and other machines can be recycled too.

There are many different types of natural metals. To be useful, they need to be separated from the rocks they're found in. Some metals are then mixed together. This creates strong, man-made metals. Some metals break up into smaller pieces but never go away. Others break down from corrosion. Corrosion is when **oxygen** combines with metal surfaces and sometimes weakens them. Warm air and water can speed up corrosion. Some metals have paint or coatings that protect them from corrosion.

oxygen gas that is needed for many things on Earth, including breathing and breaking things down

Rusting is a form of corrosion.

Metal tins are a common piece of rubbish. Many food tins are made of thin steel. They can take 50 years to break up. Aluminium is a light metal. Many drinks cans are made of it. It takes 200 to 500 years to break up.

FACT

People in the UK use more than 16 billion aluminium drinks cans every year.

Electronic devices such as computers often contain metals. Smartphones are made of a combination of metal, glass and plastic. This takes a long time to break up. When thrown away, electronics can also be dangerous.

Often, electronics contain **toxic** materials. They have chemicals that are dangerous to living things. These toxins may leak out of the devices and seep into the ground. Some landfills have systems to collect and get rid of **leachate**. But lots of electronic waste is not thrown away properly. Or there might be a tear in the landfill lining. Leachate can harm animals, plants and people nearby.

toxic poisonous or potentially harmful
leachate mixture of toxins that seep out of electronics and into the soil

ESTIMATED TIME TO DECOMPOSE OR BREAK UP

PAPER

6 weeks to decompose

WOOL CLOTHING

5 years to decompose

STYROFOAM

50+ years to break up

ALUMINIUM

200–500 years to break up

PLASTIC BAG

450 years to break up

GLASS

1 million years to break up

CHAPTER **FOUR**

HOW RUBBISH AFFECTS EARTH

People sometimes throw fast food rubbish out of car windows and onto the street. Styrofoam containers and plastic bags blow away with the wind. One piece of rubbish may not seem like it matters. But litter adds up around the world.

Every year, countries around the world are creating millions of tonnes of waste. A little more than half of this ends up in landfills.

FACT Cigarettes are the most common litter in the ocean. Plastic bottles and toys are also very common.

Litter blows around and can eventually end up in a body of water.

Rubbish that is not thrown away becomes litter. Litter pollutes Earth. Pollution is when human activity makes land, water or air dirty and unsafe. Pollution harms all plants and animals.

When rubbish is not thrown away correctly, it often ends up in the ocean. Rain and rivers carry litter from land to bodies of water.

Plastic litter is a major problem in oceans. It breaks into tiny pieces of plastic, but it doesn't go away. Some animals eat it by accident.

Rubbish with holes can get caught around an animal's neck.

WORLD'S LARGEST RUBBISH COLLECTION

A collection of plastic rubbish is floating in the ocean between California and Hawaii, USA. It is called the Great Pacific Garbage Patch. It is made of more than 1.8 trillion pieces of rubbish. Most of the rubbish is tiny pieces of plastic. The patch weighs around 80,000 tonnes and is three times the size of France!

Fish are being surrounded by toxic water. Scientists estimate that at least 5.25 trillion pieces of plastic rubbish are in the ocean.

Rubbish needs to be thrown away or recycled correctly. It can take hundreds to millions of years to break up. In that time, it can pollute environments and harm living things.

FACT

About 80 per cent of plastic in the ocean was first thrown away or littered on land.

GLOSSARY

absorb take in water

compost recycle organic matter so it becomes fertile soil

decompose break down into smaller pieces

fertile having lots of nutrients to help plants grow better

leachate mixture of toxins that seep out of electronics and into the soil

litter throw rubbish in a place where it does not belong, allowing it to end up in water or on land

microorganism living thing that is too small to be seen without a microscope

mineral material found in nature that is not an animal or plant

organic made of material that was once living

oxygen gas that is needed for many things on Earth, including breathing and breaking things down

pollute make water, air or land dirty and potentially harmful to living things nearby

silica part of sand

sodium carbonate chemical that can be used to make glass

toxic poisonous or potentially harmful

FIND OUT MORE

BOOKS

How Effective is Recycling? (Earth Debates), Catherine Chambers (Raintree, 2016)

This Book Is Not Rubbish: 50 Ways to Ditch Plastic, Reduce Rubbish and Save the World!, Isabel Thomas (Wren & Rook, 2018)

What a Load of Rubbish: What happens to the things we throw away? (The Story of Sanitation), Riley Flynn (Raintree, 2019)

WEBSITES

www.bbc.co.uk/bitesize/clips/zwywmnb
Find out what to do with your rubbish!

www.dkfindout.com/uk/science/materials/recycling-materials
Learn more about how materials are recycled.

COMPREHENSION QUESTIONS

1. Rubbish that is thrown away ends up at a landfill. Landfills can be helpful and harmful. What is one reason landfills are not the best place to put rubbish? What is one reason landfills are good for people and Earth?

2. Rubbish decomposes differently depending on what it is and where it lands. Choose one type of rubbish and describe how it decomposes. Use evidence from the text to support your answer.

INDEX